chasing ghosts

M.Z. Ribalow

NeoPoiesis Press

NeoPoiesis Press
P.O. Box 38037
Houston, TX 77238-8037

www.neopoiesispress.com

M.Z. Ribalow – Chasing Ghosts
ISBN 978-0-9832747-3-5 (paperback : alk. paper)
      1. Poetry. I. Ribalow, M.Z.

Printed in the United States of America.

First Edition

For Dasha, Patricia, Sam and Spencer,
who have always been there,
steadfast, lovely, loyal and true

Contents

"People speak of not being able to outrun their ghosts, but for me, it was just the opposite. I always felt as if I couldn't quite catch up to mine."

Alethea Black, "The Far Side of the Moon"

Scars Don't Tan

It takes so little for the unraveling to
commence – a careless gesture, a reassuring
phrase never quite uttered, a heedless
moment that seemed rhapsodically hopeful
but which left resonant repercussions that
altered everything. A legacy of scars:
emotional ones fade but not away,
physical ones blend but don't tan.

The rap music you give as a birthday gift
to your nephew because it's what he likes,
the visit you force yourself to make because
your relatives need cheering up, your friend's
neurotic phone call that consumes the night –
the recipients are grateful, but none of it
ever washes away your secret detritus.
Expiation seems a goal, but is a way of life.

It began happening so long ago, in details too
nuanced to notice. A slight misstep sprains an
ankle that never fully heals; a dropped stitch
subtly renders imperfect the entire tapestry.
Nothing to be done now but to recover; make
the most of what remains, the best of what
may be. Though you recall the white whale,
do not pursue him through the oceanic past.

Vampire

Sinking my teeth deep into you,
I feel no guilt.
You knew I was coming.
You knew your neck was bare.
I chew, tasting warm flesh,
sipping thick dark blood mouthfuls
at leisure. There's no one here to stop me.

Watching you twitch,
I feel no pain.
The bleeding body
is yours, not mine.
Not at all mine.

I never knew for sure how much you knew;
were you my victim, or my willing sacrifice?
When we were together, it was an important question.
But not now. Now you're a carcass.
My carcass. You're dead meat I eat.
All that matters now is my appetite.

Sanctuary

It begins with
a primal scream
because we haven't
yet heard the joke.

We lurch into life,
blinking, startled. We
didn't know it was a
womb until we left it.

We take a look around and
whistle, watch the sparrows
as they fly by, wonder if
there's a plot to this story.

Whatever we discover, Nature
thought of it first. Mother
Nature, we call her, even as
we make her our battered wife.

The sun teaches us to waltz
and rumba, lights our terrors,
massages us with heat. It
does not demand sacrifice.

The moon guards our
orbit, plays with tides,
reflects its searchlight
on this spinning planet.

The stars, scattered like
rice at a wedding, hang out
in the sky and wonder what
all the fuss is about.

The bear nuzzling for honey,
the snow-specked wolf, the wary

cat, find each other curious;
only humans question reality.

Souls harbor demons, shadows
that whisper and haunt our
blood. The way to overcome
a fear is to embrace it.

Risk is natural, stability
isn't. The search for sanctuary
takes us past red lights, smiling
strangers, loves we don't understand.

Our passions are who we
are, the dreams our dreams
dream of, the butterfly
of our crawling caterpillar.

Life is a rough draft,
never ready for itself.
The only style that makes
any sense is celebration.

Symmetry is not harmony.
Parallel bars were meant
to be uneven. To live is
to constantly reconsider.

Give and take. Joined,
harmonious unison;
separate, just two
four-letter words.

The mind can make an apple
of a desert, turn a garden
into a favorite novel.
Perspective is everything.

The magician asked God
how to levitate without
trickery. "Don't come
down," said God.

It's all natural magic:
a baseball game, an
act of love, the odd
inexplicable mystery.

One man's oatmeal is
another woman's science-
fiction. We are mostly
water, but partly irony.

If we can speak, we can
sing. If we can move,
we can dance. We are the
answer to our prayers.

We choose our paths, seek
shelter from our storms.
But only within ourselves
will we find sanctuary.

The Feather

A feather floats from above
descends somewhere south of heaven
rises, falls, seeks convergence with her
path, glides to a pause before she arrives

So many disembodied words skim and slide
cleave through the ethereal air yearning
for connection, for paradise never fully lost,
the quiet ache that is its own heartbeat

There, at the turning point of the still world
the merest sound echoes, broken strings
resound within their own vibrating silence,
the here and now, the ever and always

Days flee from nights, invisible tracks trace
graceful sorrows seeking light that might
comfort, might dance with darkling stars, make
the holy sacred. The feather stirs, not yet moved.

A Poem (of sorts) About Her

She makes Venus de Milo look like an armless statue.

She makes all the things that haven't changed seem
different.

I want to read *Alice In Wonderland* with her.
Also Chandler and Runyon.

I want to dive deep into the seas of her fathomless
eyes.

I know a squillion people must have used that
metaphor, but it still feels original.

I have seen the grass look happier when she went by.

I taste her as a thirsty plant tastes water.

As long as her eyes look like that, the world has its
points.

To be with her is to reach a destination.

This sentence eternally admires her.

This sentence is plenty skeptical, but will go along
for now.

This sentence adores her with unrestrained passion.

This sentence feels rather the same way, but is trying
to be cool about it.

She assures me that being this beautiful wasn't
her idea.

Whosever idea it was, I offer congratulations
and thanks.

She can make walking across a room an act of grace.

She isn't really more exquisite than a white rose.
It only seems that way.

To write a poem about her is redundant.

If there is a God, he must have smiled when he made
her.

I think about her whenever snow falls. Also whenever
it doesn't.

I want to spend a day in bed with her reading *King
Lear.*

I want to spend days in bed with her not reading *King
Lear.*

Wherever she is, is where I'd rather be than here.

She is less breathtaking than an Arizona sunset.
But not by much.

She is earth and air, comprehended mystery,
explicable magic, perfect in her imperfection.

That last sentence is prejudiced. But also true.

She is a sweet ache strumming softly behind my eyes.

She is a gift, to be taken only when given.

She is herself.

Heritage

When I spit black fire
it's the Jew in me;
Israel's inexorable child
baked dark under two thousand
nomad suns, tolerated
in the promised land,
always different,
always Jew.

I may love you.
But now and then
my eyes narrow watching
you (my God, even you)
because I know that
somewhere, sometime
your blood has tasted mine
and mine is hungry.

Another Nighttime Love Poem

Somewhere in this darkened room a clock ticks.
There it sits upon the stony mantelpiece, an
impassive hunk of graven wood for my carved
company. The silent sounds of deepening night
melt into morning.

All too far away dreams a woman who may
or may not conjure me this musing moment
as I do her. Her face hovers before me like
December breath: constantly reappearing
without ever quite departing.

There are words to say that have been
said. She is not quite close enough to
hear them just now; but they are said
anyway, silently, to her, for her.
Sometimes suddenly

the slightest shadow of her image leaps
at me from nowhere's somewhere, and
the odd tidal wave sweeps over my
semi-startled self. The night moves
its imperturbable way.

Dawn will soon yawn lazily in the
encompassing sky. But at this still
moment, nothing inside this room
alters but the clock's hands and my
remembering body.

Someone Slipped

Someone slipped
Whoops there goes
Another cartwheel
Spins around so
Amazingly so
Maybe it was
Me or she
In a moment
Of musing on my
My oh my well
Slipped on an
Invisible (they
Sometimes are)
Banana peel
You never know
For sure
What she thinks
I can guess
I think
About her
Now and then
Here and there
All at once
She comes
And goes
When she will
She does
Does she ever
Consider that
Since that day
And night times
Are not the
Same old familiar
What they were
They aren't
Bad at all
She does is

Okay with
Me as is
She is somewhat
Wonderful not
A bad way to
Be around her
It's rather nice
To slip when
One lands so
Near her so
Far so good
So nice so
Someone slipped
So what
Could be
Much nicer
Than that show
Me that peel
Off the rest
Will be so
Fine with
Me as is
She
Is
So
Fine

Macbeth

Soldier, you should not have
swallowed so much blood.
We sacrifice our vampires
our Technicolor monsters
our King Kongs,
Lee Harvey Oswalds.
Your severed head
stuck on a stake
competes for Nielsen ratings.

Astrologers whisper dark omens.
Each night, a bad moon rises;
your ghosts appear, a row
of raw bleeding ulcers.
Your insomniac wife will
drop dead in the last act.
Nothing is left but a front-page death
so you brought your rifle to the roof
and murdered pedestrians.

You should have watched out
for those weird sisters,
witches sharp as computers.
Clickety-clack, prophecies
spun off precise as IBM cards.
Spectres instead of statistics.
They invest in apparitions.
Do not fold, bend or mutilate.
These things will happen.

Still, Life

She writes. Time wrings her like a rag
made of words while she rings Time
in return, capturing it on the page in
small, roundly perfect anomalies that
will outlive her (and me) even as they
define the very life they describe.
Time is discomfited and rhapsodic
being so possessed, and so is she.

Her life is pictures at an exhibition:
a series of recalled moments available
for perusal by the unknown friend.
One may now meet her with an intimacy
mocking convention, as when I myself
dated Dickinson and married Millay.
With words she justifies her creation.
Where there is God, she would be his will.

Hylas and the Nymphs

There are seven of them
in the painting, but they
are all identical. Tumbling
tresses drift loosely,
waterfall cascades frame
dreamy pre-Raphaelite features.
Each nymph cloned from another

Each hypnotic glance a
silently eloquent echo
of her sister stares. None
of these multiple maidens
preceded each other; one
pure spellbinding spirit
suffuses each sister soul.

Of course they are inseparably
same to the dazzled youth. Of
course. Perfection times seven.
He grows drunk with realized
fantasy of a seven-bodied nymph
who will drown his dark beauty
in her still, silent spring.

They will him to them. Enter
the water, cries the siren call.
One pleads. Others cajole, demand,
yearn, wish, beckon. One seems
indifferent. All seductive beyond
thought or reason. All her selves,
all herself. His lady of the lake.

His soul's shadow. Join us, the
eyes say simply, seven sets of
mesmerizing mirrors. Dive deep.
You have nothing to lose but your
forfeit life. You have us to gain.

Join us. Will you, won't you
join us. We have come for you.

For you alone have we come.
We can solve nothing,
but we can do it all.
Whispered words possess him.
He leans forward, hopelessly
hopeful, ready to slip into
the greenish, weeping water.

Slim pale hands reach, touch
his bare extended arm. Seven
slender bodies in single, singing
harmony. Wind keens through
serene reeds. You are one of us
now. We are all yours. You are
all ours. We are all one.

Scarecrow

Scarecrow stalks the city streets
ostentatious as the Statue of Liberty;
everyone notices, no one pays any
attention. Four children burned
themselves to deep fried crisps
in the middle of a hydrogen heist
hijack of a plague flea fresh from
research lab carrying fire flood
famine biological malfunction and
the search for tomorrow's subway.
It was quite a story. Tonight on
the six o'clock news it will join
Scarecrow and we will take it all
into account, measuring between
commercial breaks the meaning
of it all. Fathers will beget sons,
sons will be getting on with the
father business, women will wonder
and make their way. Nothing will
bear watching, but everything
will be examined minutely. All
analysis must be comprehensible,
recorded, filed for the record.
Scarecrow is as indifferent to
all this as a pole vaulter to the
Dead Sea Scrolls. Data is what
he drinks, so much orange juice
or blood. He does not discriminate.
His straw bones may burn and
blacken, but will not go away.
He comes, when he comes, to
stay. Cameras will linger on the
charred skeletal shape, but not
for long. Old news pales quickly.
The freak becomes known, common,
banal in turn. No less crippled,
killer still, but reassuringly familiar.

Armageddon is scheduled as next
week's television spectacular. It
has lost its terror. Scarecrow grins
but not at that. He can do nothing
else, expression fixed as a totalitarian
election. He knows no pleasure.
He has no need to understand
anything. He is Scarecrow. That
is sufficient. Lives, televisions,
all is forfeit. So put down your
money and pick a card. Any card.
Scarecrow will call all bets.

Flight

Peering through the airplane window
at the tiny pointillist dots below
shows me what the gods must see.
But not what they know; because
we are none of us more than mortal,
profoundly ignorant of ourselves.

Those suffused with certitude seem
enviable in their surety, but the
stupidity of smugness taints the very
notion of conviction. The search for
The Holy Grail is meaningless if you
think you already bought it last Friday.

The one universal truth – that none
of us truly understands anything –
escapes them. They constantly convince
themselves they recognize what they
see; they need to know their place
so as to be sure that they have one.

The road traveled is as mysterious
as is the one not taken. Water
is more magical than card tricks.
The only consistency lies in paradox.
I fly through the sky looking down
at myself still below, gazing up.

Under My Skin

Every day I don't send you a letter
I write to you. The hours we do not speak
I talk with you. Each moment you're away
I see you close to me. The words you don't
hear whispered are the ones I'm saying now.
I feel you as a dolphin feels the sea.
I touch you as a banker touches gold.
The absence of your presence hovers over me
like the high sky. All the world's wisdom is a
melted snowflake at the breathless sight of you.
I cannot not want you. I will not not love you.
You are the kiss of life.

Self-Portrait

Not mine. Rembrandt's.
Mine must be in words.
Paint still strange to me
as nuclear physics; the
results may be breathtaking,
but the process is mysterious
as a unicorn. Much easier
for me to understand
baseball, or murder.

He seems to know more,
this master of light and shade
whose quizzical stare hangs
on an Amsterdam wall. He is
no prosperous merchant benign
as the Secretary of State. His
shrewd dark eyes have seen
too many fools. He knows
how much he does not know.

In Holland, as in Jerusalem,
monuments are feverishly
erected. Fires burn and turn
to ash. A baby cries on his
way to the grave. This is the
way it has been, and will be.
So it goes. He seems aware
of it all, this gentle, sad-eyed
man who has suffered, this

friend of the Jews. No contempt
here for the well-fed bourgeoisie
who would never understand the
blinding yellow pain that drove
Van Gogh to split his sun in two.
This reflected Rembrandt knew,

this brooding master of souls;
but he just mused, and drew faces
with chiaroscuro and compassion.

Icarus

It's the ultimate trick.
To reach a peak
stay there then
rise higher, ever
higher, and not
fall, and not
disintegrate.
No party trick
of this wild world's
carnival demands more
delicate balance, such
finely tuned wire on
the tightrope act.
Slip and you crash.
Go too high and you
melt into fragments.

Icarus learned that fate
too late, the hard way,
the sun too seductive
a shimmering drug
too brightly blinding.
Golden quivers mainlined
their acid way into
his bubbling blood
smacked his addicted
self into stunned
scattered sundust
all the brain's grains
diffusely swept
every which way
through the suction
of the universe.

As his wax wings bled
from soaring too high
his body plummeted,

neatly detached now
from his doomed speed's
sense. He dropped into
drowning waters that
waited to suck him
into oblivion.
Disembodied ecstasy
left a vaporized trail
across his fall. The
gritty roughness of
reality vanished,
banished into the great
multicolored extravaganza
of his sunburst consciousness,
that terrific tumbling act
ever so abruptly
forever cancelled.
All over now
the wondrous visions
that danced in the high sky
where his mind once was.

Carrot Curls

for Rhona

There is craft involved in the cooking.
Not only time (overdone means doing
over; underdone, uncurled orange pieces
resist irresistibility) but also an urge
to create them perfectly; the passionate
pride in doing it well because it requires
doing. This is what he can consume;
thus it is needful to ladle love with skill.

These crisped strips must become
the like of French fries because
they are so much more than that.
His besieged little body needs
nourishment that feeds the soul
recycling the circle of daily life.
His wonderment mambos with her
watchfulness while carrots sizzle.

Toubac

for Jenna

They offer her a drink and call her "toubac."
She knows it means "white girl," synonym for
rich young American slut, green card ticket.
As she works she watches horses drag carts
over potholes, a goat on a car roof. Senegal's
children watch her wide-eyed as did last year's
Mexicans. There are so many of them here,
ten or more to each struggling mother it seems.
The husbands are away for months, working;
so wives sleep with men in the village for food.

Heat blankets her senses with oppressive weight
while a man tells her how much females cannot
understand. A woman balances a jar on her head;
another carefully weaves something mysterious
that is sure to be useful. A wild bird shrieks
in the distance; a turbaned shepherd ushers
his flock of goats across the road. The sun
slinks into the west, knowing it will be followed
by a starry cloth across the sky's table. The
white girl will fall asleep before she will rest.

The Bear

for N. Scott Momaday

God used both hands
when he made the bear.

Musing, he wades into
the swirling waters
that roar and beckon,
the torrent of sounds.

He washes his paws
and fur and spirit.

Days, he feels the sun's
heat, looks at what
its light illuminates.
Nights, he lurches at
the moon, calls it sister
and lover, reaches for it.

Listen. You can hear him
in his forest, thrashing
through the trees, unafraid
of the noise he makes.

He wonders what makes
the wind play with his

grizzled, hungry body.
Sometimes he sleeps,
at peace with his
passions and appetites,

and dreams of his snout
dripping with honey.

Soldier's Birthday

I wish myself a happy birthday
while a man bleeds to death
in the back of my helicopter.
I will spend my twenty-first year
hoping I live to be twenty-two.
Send me a present. Please do.
I hear there's a purpose to all these
grinning skulls, these dead babies.
Mail me a postcard
with a picture of heaven.

I have nothing to give a woman.
I have only bullets and words.
Bullets are deaf. Disinterested.
Words rot in my mouth like rancid candy.
I am weary, weary of dying every day.
A woman's breasts are the only
weapons I want to hold.

Anyone I don't shoot may murder me.
Send me a card. It's my birthday.
At twenty-one years, I am a soldier.
A killer of men. I understand nothing
I know. I see too many children
whose eyes are ashes.

Tiger in the Tree

He waits with the serene
patience of a natural hunter,
driven by an eternal hunger.

His saber-toothed smile
aches for your neck,
longs to bite lovingly.

You shudder as you contemplate
the erotic, penetrating embrace.
You tell yourself insistently

You want security, not teeth
on the nape of your neck.
After all, what if they

Darken your blood so you
despair of emerging into
bright, sufficient light?

Might the mad, sad, lovely
beast be your destruction?
Or salvation? After all?

You approach the tree, pretend
obliviousness to the hot eyes
that eat you from a distance.

You wander away, hoping to be
followed, but terrified of
being consumed. You know

The difference between
fulfillment of fantasy
and fantasy fulfilled.

The tiger stays still in the
tree, obvious, hidden. His
stare burns through leaves.

You imagine, despite yourself,
his rough, licking tongue on
your shy, voracious flesh.

Would your heartbeats merge?
Would their drumming duet of
passion fade – and into what?

A steady beat? A lifelong set
of bravura riffs, reveling in
syncopation, rhythm, nuance?

He wants your touch; you want
his heart under your small
hands. He conjures your breath

Blending into his; you yearn
for the taste of that raspy
tongue. He dreams of possession,

You of being possessed. He longs
to be captive captor; you feel
sweet power of shared surrender.

Could you live within those
claws, those paws, that
constant rippling appetite?

Would you live without it?
Predator, lover, pursuer of
your body, stalker of your soul:

He watches and waits, animal
composure powerfully helpless,
forbiddingly irresistible.

You leave him in his shrouded,
leafy exile, amazed he doesn't
go away, knowing he will stay.

The Eighth Deadly Sin

Despair.
The deepest-dyed of all.
Lust horrifies mostly those
who resent its giddy appeal
Greed lacks spirituality
Sloth wants discipline
Still all of them seem
somehow surmountable
But not Despair
not the one that
so terrified the priests
they left it out of
the cosmic equation.
Of them all
Despair is the greatest sin
because it feeds the need
to inflict the decaying
corpses of one's own
bitterly drowned hopes
upon everyone else.

Suicide Note

They sent me photos of the hanging.
I don't remember you as being pretty;
and even in romantic suicides,
corpses rarely show to advantage.
The police thoughtfully enclosed
a copy of your final note as well.
I wondered why you made me next-of-kin.
It only lasted seven weeks, or less.

Even then your life was wasted:
not empty, but tasteless, like bad sex,
obscenely apathetic. Now it's all over:
the bad debts, the strange beds, the awful hush.

Now you lie flat
iced in the city morgue
waiting for burial.
Of all your sneering men,
your surly two-week lovers
who never liked you,
what made you pick on me
as you scribbled?

Parents wonder where
you are, how you're doing,
their wistful smiles proud
as they sit around the living
room browsing through
your high school yearbook.

Pilgrim's Progress

The scalps of a million redskins have
atrophied on the prairies, now thick
with wavy wheat and corn harvested
by machines from Detroit when the
workers quit their next strike. They
don't know what they've missed,
these ghosts of haunted hunters,
but Geronimo might have guessed.
Another shiny space probe rockets
through the galaxy, zips the unsuspecting
stars a bit tighter into our pockets.
Machine guns stutter briskly in Africa.
Concern trickles from national capitols
like lukewarm coffee, real but tasteless.
It happens every day, they say.
Sure it's terrible, but it's no big deal.
Babies down nutritional chemicals,
beauty queens who play harmonicas
and chess are crowned in Miami Beach.
The death of rabbits may or may not one
day find a cure for cancer. Nations
debate over ownership of rainclouds
that hover above, stormy but impassive.
The entrails of the rabbits, humors of
the clouds used to be read as foretelling
omens. They still serve as instruments.
Governments are throne and overthrown.
Medicine improves as rapidly as
people get sicker. Surveys prove
definitively that statistics supply
figures. Comets zoom by, take a look
and get out of town pronto.
Ozymandias has bought the planet
with the fortune he made in oil.
Reconstructions of constructions
are under way. Before we're quite
finished, a sequel is being planned.

Spirits whisper over the Dakota plains
when no one is there to eavesdrop.

God, interviewed in Atlanta, admits
he may have miscalculated slightly.

Pay the Piper

Delicate strains lace the air;
the piper waves mass choruses
past paved streets, harvested
fields, to the sea. The shores
seem to shine beneath the piper's
soaring chords. When the piper's
liquid rhythm flows, we are grateful.

Isn't it a pity his melody lobotomizes,
puts fresh linen on the deathbed,
livens the wake. Isn't it a pity
the piper's music disinfects
the sweet reek of mortality.
Isn't it a blessing.

You gaily lead children to ocean's
edge, gaily watch them drown.
You light women like cigarettes,
exhale broken smoke,
light another match.

Beautiful black-eyed bastard,
your fluty tune spellbinds us all.
Your music washes away final silence,
but only briefly. For you I have a
declaration: deep love, but no forgiveness,
uncrowned king of the hill, melodious killer.

Listen to the tune of the bloodsucking angel,
but remember: the piper must be paid.
On the way out, pay the piper.

Bottle Caps

on Monday morning I look at my
green and blue and red and yellow
bottle caps lined up neatly on my
dresser you may say that they have
no real function but I know you can't
deny that they are neat on Tuesday
I don't even look I don't have to I
know they're there the truth is only
sometimes with – well, you know –
do I wonder, in the flip side of the night,
if I'm young enough to die or blond
enough to go back home again
fortunately this happens less and less
these days and on Mondays I look at my
green and blue and red and yellow bottle caps

A Wound

They call this
a wound. It
throbs, bleeds, aches.
It is vulnerable.

Go on, touch
it. It is
yours. It is
all yours.

It's the natural
order of things,
this damp
red lump.

Yes, if you squeeze,
it will crush like
a cigarette pack.
Disposable. Used.

I won't bandage
this sore. It won't
heal without your touch.
Yours to cripple, or cure.

They have other
names for it,
this stubborn scar,
but love will do.

Jigsaw

If sometimes from the total
puzzle's picture a bit may
seem detached, it isn't.
It just hasn't yet snapped
fully into place completing
all those other patient pieces.

The jigsaw can seem peaceful,
intriguing, alarming, seductive,
possessed in turn. It can be all
of those and more. Fair enough.
That's what makes puzzles puzzling.

But what if each and every distinctly
different chunk contains within it
a jagged edge of a helpless, hungry
keen waiting, wishing to be loosed.

If you like – if you really want to –
you can put your ear to a jigsaw part
and listen. Listen carefully if you
would hear it weep and sing.

The Supper

"Thou hast committed fornication – but that was in another country, and besides, the wench is dead." –Christopher Marlowe

"Knowledge begins with what the senses tell us. From this we may abstract an idea of the world, which is a fiction. These fictions and inventions are also our truths." –Wallace Stevens

I. SETTING THE TABLE

Cattycorner from sole concerns
the table within the house is spread
with shining pieces of silver
in the patient dinging donging dining room.
The house is subject to the sun (opposed to darkness)
if one may, fairly, object, wind
the winding sheet of the peaceful wake away from
the windows by Tim Finnegan's soaking singing body.
Finnegan, lying cheerfully by drawn shades,
makes his own profit and will not be at supper.

Unlike the rest. Supper set, the Cook's dinner
party
is present
five men are there
a woman
the picture of a girl
and the Cook is in the kitchen.
The Cook is always in the kitchen.

II. DICHOTOMIES AND DIRECTIONS

Black Jack heaves himself splashing from the
bathtub,

40

rubbing himself clean with his busy hands,
praying to himself,
"arma feminasque meumque cano, qui semper amo..."

Black Jack has the use of both his eyes,
has no wish to be the King of Clubs
or any other of the pack.
He reaches for the flesh that Madame clothed in velvet
has,
murdering plurally of a creaking night,
resurrected past the yawning of the morning.
Black Jack shaves
himself
in the morning
when he shaves,
is carefully unshaven every night,
wears no tie and carries none.

Madame clothed in silk slides tightly into the room
colors of the sea reflected
in her conscious eyes
tickling the five the scarecrow did not have
to sense death's other kingdom,
"For mine is the power,
and the glory,
today
and tomorrow..."

The one-eyed guitar picker
has his guitar to pick,
pays some or no attention to what he is to eat
composing his chords, speaking to his voice
"Reality is a crutch and truth is an illusion."
The one-eyed guitar picker plays a song
forgetting the food on the table
eating the strains, tinted melodious chords
of polished blue, the music charming
Madame clothed in warm-weather cotton,
her skirt pushed back above her thighs,

her flesh soft, warm and patient around
Black Jack's busy hand.
She waits for the one-eyed guitar picker
to look up;
but he, too, is playing.

Away outside
the red-eyed elders giggle at their clavichords,
the Red Baron
before he even comes to supper
conducting the direction of their chants.
The Baron stands
solid
stolid
dry
crackling
at times when he is touched.
He is no swinger of birches.
From the sticks cut from the tree's branches
he demands punishment atop the red rock.

In the dining room,
the Thin Jew stands a starved and helpless prisoner
of the rusty red-eyed Baron
who wears his pious blue and white
though only his undershorts are blue
and barely shaded.
The Baron's temples are scarred;
he wears his iron cross about his neck
and holds a full-time job.

The Thin Jew mourns his faith
lost in intensity
doubted in belief
destroyed by acceptance.

The Thin Jew has a picture of his father
standing
erect

full beard flowing freely to his feet,
cold-eyed, praying,
talisman for what exists
hard to recognize.

The Thin Jew has a picture of his mother
dressed,
though he has seen her naked
smiling gently at Leonardo's jests.

The Thin Jew has a picture of himself, but
he cannot find it.

The Cook spoils the broth,
keeping the ingredients of his omelet hidden
breaking eggs
cracking out the yolks from eggshells,
washing down the gulped devoured food
with a piece of bread
a glass of vintage blood-red wine
marking the meal kosher.
Dichotomies are clear in opposition
and little else;
if the Cook prepared the dinner,
why does the food invariably rot?
The cook has a fine sense of humor,
and we eat his meals –
but he is the only cook around,
we cannot judge him in comparison.

The King of Clubs rules over a kingdom
(Prometheus is unbound
but crippled)
and here he comes fast
to feast
plodding to the table harshly.

All in the dining-room dream of the girl-child,
even Madame clothed in pink chiffon

who does not favor females
and the King of Clubs who is not given to dreaming.
Her picture is always on the wall,
though none have ever seen herself in visit.

The one-eyed guitar picker mostly does the dreaming,
though Black Jack yearns
and the King of Clubs heaves a heavy breath
in her direction, and the Thin Jew
looks longingly from his reddened chains.
The girl-child smiles from her picture,
milky in her hallowed peace, warm in white
each dream through which she wanders
holds the dreamer through the agony of want;
the dreams of his hands on her hips,
young smoothed thighs, unguarded breasts,
beneath her flowing white.
To each, his planting would be serene as she,
the soil being virgin unpossessed.
They all believe that
except possibly the Thin Jew
who is condemned and says nothing.
Perhaps he too believes.
The Cook knows better, who has lain with her,
himself huge inside her groin, becoming it,
fingers wound in her Porphyria's hair.
How could those terrified vague fingers
protest what they're created to receive?
She is a nymphomaniac, her appetite swollen
by the deferential worship she receives.
Her halo is the pillow of her bed,
but only in the kitchen with the Cook
and no one else can know.
All stare at the picture, patient, in admiration.

III. DINNER

The table is full, the food provided by
the King of Clubs, prepared by the Cook.
The King of Clubs unleashes his heavy
cudgeled power upon the animals he finds,
destroying what is perishable.
There is a tempting fish holding promises
though often eaters are gilled into breathing
what is not wholly air.
Thick pork there is, two rounded halves
around the cutting knife;
a boar's flesh, heavy, juiced and salted;
cabbage filled with undefined but vaguely familiar
stuffing within the leaves.
There is also a dead bird.

The Red Baron consumes the fish with wine,
has crackers for dessert, eating steadily,
unaware what is on other plates.
Madame clothed in a red sheet
seizes the plate of pork,
clutches the knife tightly, twitching
to Black Jack's ringing rampant laughter
around the round table as
she stuffs her mouth and groans.
The King of Clubs eats
hearty, subliminally conscious,
tongue rasping over the boar's flesh
all but raw
washing down the gravied blood
with a piece of soft white bread.
His Adam's apple gulps what he consumes
eating, not knowing what is eaten, eating,
eating, just eating, just that, eating.

The one-eyed guitar picker
pokes within the stuffing of the cabbage,
picking

placing
eating
to find what is within the flaps
of draping cabbage leaves,
and know what is digested.

The one-eyed guitar picker is accused
by the King of Clubs' stare
by Black Jack's hand upon the leg
of Madame clothed in animal hides
of leaving food upon his plate.
He argues for alternatives to this.

"We left much more, left what is still
the look of things,
left what we felt at what we saw."

Black Jack laughs and fills his plate
heaping, spilling over the brim,
food to be consumed, bellyful
through tongue and teeth,
laughing as he eats, mouth full.
Jack the bubbler drinks without
compunction or compassion
secure in what he does not need to know.
About around attack on the meat,
Teeth in and out, over and under and in,
swilling the liquor, eating the bread,
devouring the meat, drinking the wine.
His appetite is not at all disgusted or displaced
by his or others' retching at the meal.
"It's part," he says, "of our digestive process."
He drinks his tea
and swallows the sugar cube whole.

The Red Baron eats and does not listen,
never having heard of Crazy Jane.

46

The Thin Jew gets the bird,
and looks hungry.

The Cook sits frostily upon his stool,
well above the stove, and eats nothing
being full.

IV. CLEARING THE TABLE

The company whispers around the table merrily
the Cook stays in the kitchen
smiling
and the night nears its end.
The monster slouching towards Bethlehem
has footsteps of a tiger, eyes that burn bright,
in or out
caught or freed
in red weather
under a blue sky
over green earth.

Boozing It

This is some bar, this is.
His hair slicked down with too much wildroot
(parted in the middle)
Buddha hustles billiards with his ebony cue,
sweat patching his pinstriped shirt,
eyes impassive above his thick cigar.
Pale hands grip the lean stick and
crack! clack! crack!
The balls obediently slide across
the felt and sink.
Her hair bleached,
smooth skin looking slightly used,
Aphrodite croons in the shadow of the sailor's arms
while he sprawls in the corner.
One hand strokes his face;
slim jeweled fingers of the other
slip towards his pocket.
A poet reels on a wooden table,
spouting drunken verse and foamy beer.
Torrential words stagger on his ailing tongue:
rich, bursting, incomprehensible.
Pericles, elder statesman of the town,
bribes the bartender, sips wine;
Babe Ruth of South Central High
watches happily, knocking back tequila
while the rabbitman marks time.
Christ the Butcher swings his cleaver,
hacks at chicken liver in the parlour.
The bar is crowded, murky;
voices flow like running water.
"Have a drink!" someone shouts.
"Take your place and have a drink."
I weave through swaying bodies,
heading for the spirits at the bar.

In Dreams

From your sleeping neck I lick
a drop of sweat. You stir slightly,
your dreams jostled. Will she smile,
I wonder, and you do, fleetingly.

Are your dreams so sweet, then? Or is
there some secret sleeping knowledge
that you possess, or that possesses
you? Can you keep it when you wake?

Our clothes lie scattered on the rug like
a teenage trail. Chopin plays softly on the
CD we never turned off. Had it been Roy
Orbison instead, would it have mattered?

I lie awake, watching your ear, your cheek,
your lips, imagining ways to torture you
with pleasure. You are turned away, yet
I feel your skin breathe under my own.

We all have our secrets.
Some of yours I know.
You yourself are mine.

Leftover Pieces

Not until tonight did I
look through the bag you
brought me. A Macy's bag.
A big one. With handles.

A bag full of last effects,
like the metal box in
the morgue after
they've iced the body.

Cards, letters, photos, one neat
bundle of emotional laundry;
a smell of bittersweet nostalgia,
like an outgrown baseball glove.

That Viking dress I always
loved you in. The purple
flowered print you never
wore except for me.

My throat feels like I've
swallowed a dull razor.
It's two a.m. I'm exhausted.
I wish I could sleep.

I stare at that gorgeous
handpainted Ukrainian
Easter egg, so exquisite,
so extravagantly breakable.

When I saw it in the shopping
bag I wondered why you
hadn't smashed it. Or kept it.
Now it's unbroken but lost.

Outcast objects banished from
their natural home. Last week

we orphaned them. They huddle
mutely in their paper prison.

It's all become so specific. A
lifetime tossed into a shopping
bag. Contents I cannot buy
or sell. Priceless. Useless.

You've shed all our
mementoes, so many
snakeskins out of season.
Souvenirs of last year's miracles.

The shopping bag silently ticks
in the corner, a delicate time
bomb. I don't dare touch it.
My fingers might explode.

If I look into it at the
wrong moment I'm
afraid I might see my
own head, severed.

The air in this room has
shattered into fragments.
They surround me, leftover
pieces of a fallen sky.

Her Poem

I never wrote her a poem.
I don't know why not.
I was aware of the absence.

I remember the lovely sturdiness
of her smooth bare arms
shirtsleeves rolled up efficiently
over sun kissed skin as she bent
to fix a flat tire, pioneer determination
etched onto that small, grave face.
She liked Elizabethan music,
liked to have her ear lobes pulled.
I always reached for ways
to prompt the sudden swift
startled delight of her
unexpected, unexpecting smile.

She's in another country now,
yet still more real to me than
wine that tours my tongue,
or my reflection in a mirror.

She could sit quietly for hours,
small and still, folded in a corner,
asking nothing. Expecting nothing.
Willing herself into invisibility.
I can still see her huddled
so deceptively still, all the while
bleeding slowly, steadily from
internal, fiercely silent wounds.
Miracle cures are no miracles.
Someone has figured out a way.
But all those unnursed lacks
throbbed on, as painfully dangerous
as shattered glass caught in the throat.

She needed more from me
than she got. Where was I?
Where did I think I was?

She would knock down a wall
if she had to,
then build the wall back up.
She could make a song
soar into lonely flight,
a melancholy nightingale.
She could take four broken sticks
and make of them a home.
She could make the world
all right.
She was herself, her own poem.
I might seek one different.
I will never find one more.

Abortion

Your tickertape chatter
offers candy compliments on
my wit, my great good humor.
Your frozen words crack and smoke,
dry ice bouncing off these white walls.
Your teeth grind out a seasick smile.

I know you mean well.
After all, you got the money.
You will leave these cool corridors
whispering to others how well I am taking it.
Someday you will marry a pleased virgin.
You will make the transition.

Inside I am scraped clean.
Oddly detached from your solicitous
grief, small waves of proud relief.
This jeering pain in my intestines
is far more real than your glazed
eyes, your reassuring TV voice.

I am pure as the sea, a wounded
mermaid you may no longer touch.
I have eaten my young. Devoured by
a scalpel proxy for three green bills.
I have bought my own barrenness.
Beware my flesh. Beware.

Someday I will bear children.
The doctors say I need have no doubt.
But I will never be eaten again.
I am not digestible.
I will stick in your throat,
choke you like a fish bone.

I conjured wet stains on those antiseptic
sheets. I will go home soon. Darling,

54

I will make you disintegrate.
my blood is dark red acid, and you,
my vampire who poured me this dead
life, you must drink it too.

Conceptions

The child is father
       to the sin of sinning,
Father to the smoking felt within
       his ashtray soul,
Father to the rainbow after which
       he crawls, grasping
for a pot of gold.

The child's coiled birth surfaces
       through Ledaen shudders in the loins.
Squalling rude and naked,
       heaving from the
trembling spread belly,
       he emerges
a torn beginning towards an end
       dying by the days.

Epiphany

The wading girl
wet in the easy water
long hair bucketing
white hand sliding
over mermaid tresses
the boy as man
lies at night in silken dreams
falling in lust with the girl
of flesh falling in love with
the girl of the gesture that
for the rest of his semi-reversible
days he will feel remembering
with love the long-forgetting girl.

For Juliette

She shifts, breathless, from
one job, one flat, one man
to another. And another,
pausing only long enough to
toss desperate irony around,
fueling the constant humor
before it starts to fade.
Perhaps she's brave to
mock her helplessness,
but the quick despairing
laugh hides nothing.
I know that as well as she,
and I will not share her havoc;
yet I almost wish I would.
Her life is a prayer
and if I were God
(which I am not)
I would answer.

Butterfly Lady

Butterfly Lady, the world crawls with
collectors to tuck you in a bottle
stab you with a sharp edge
till the flutter stops
display your dead rainbow skin
pinned to a velvet coffin.

Little caterpillar, your thin limbs
hug each other, tentative,
search for connection.
Consider how easily one is
stepped on, squashed or
hung out to dry.

Butterfly Lady, beware
the needle killers.
I want you alive.
I want to hear your heart beat.
Shiver your delicate wings.
While you can, take flight.

Astronaut

The planet shrinks as you
fly, hangs in the heavens,
a green tennis ball tossed
away. And there you go,
careening through space,
courtesy of our limitless
ambition, trying to edge
a bit closer to the gods,
maybe make a house call.

So, this bucket of metal
and pride, better than a
flying carpet. One mistake,
one malfunction of those
shiny panels, and you've
had it – sure as any of
Odysseus's sailors eaten,
drowned or otherwise
deactivated on that trip.

Since then, you ride the
advantages of progress:
rockets, mission control,
television, vitamin B-12.
I grow exhausted as I
picture you whiz past the
stars, repress any awe.
Fear might be naked, final.
Control is a necessary illusion.

That flat language you
perfect, that dull
monotonous computerized
patter, serves as pale
makeup to cover hot
sweated flesh: the

stunned terror of where
you are and how
God let you get there.

Maybe, after all, the
cosmic joke is over
your head. You will
die soon, like the
rest of us. And no
matter what you find
out there, you won't
know what it is. And
it may not matter.

To an Unpublished Poet

Everything you do in Maine,
you do with your neighbors.
If you're a murderer,
you kill them.
If you're a poet,
you write about them,
not for love or money
but for gnawing compulsions
chewing at your liver
sidling up through your fingers
spitting wails, croons, snarls
from fevered pen to enigmatic
paper. Spewing images of
Wayne sitting in Montana
watching the trains go by
Chicago to Seattle
Seattle to Chicago;
of Ike rambling through drugstores
getting stoned on codeine.
Maine winter nights are quiet,
no more seasonal work,
not much food.
So you digest poetry,
and it consumes you.

No Fool Like a Young Fool

Being one,
I was of course the other.
Naturally.
So for many days & nights
I starved my hungry flesh
fasting loyally & stupidly
(rather relishing the classic
tradition of the role,
the easy suffering)
poured my agile words into
sixteen-page letters.
All the while
secretly knowing
that she was writing brief,
concise descriptions to
her girlfriend in Seattle.

Coming and Going

They all run busily about
hum, buzz in the frenzied
hopalong dance, each one
desperate to make a mark;
his mark, recognized as him,
definition of his oncetime
breath left identification for
the legions that may come
next. Shrill and brighteyed
is the hurly-burly hustle;
the curtain comes down
any time now, the show
must squeeze itself in.
So step right up, stay
in the wide sky's way,
the stopwatch is off
and running, you're being
timed. The case is brief.
Just the quick hour to
draw the laces tight,
spin along, make your
grab for the big brass
ring, the pie in the
sky, the solar nexus.
Take, before you drop,
the daring deep leap
to kingdom come; take
your turn to try to cast
a shadow on the sun.

Rapunzel Redux

I was always enraptured
by the streaming mane that
wraps me inside her
tumbling silken splendor.

I climb that flowing
ladder to the beckoning
window, dive recklessly
and glad headfirst into

the tower room beyond.
No castle keep, however
armed and guarded,
could keep me away.

I know
I've felt these
locks fall
over me before.

This is not the
first time I've
nested in this
particular paradise.

There is a lesson to be
learned, I know, but
here is her hair and I
hold on, for dear life.

Rapunzel, as often
as you let down
those tresses I'll
climb into them.

Acknowledgements

The following poems have been previously published:

Vampire, *The Paris Review*
The Supper, *The Literary Review*
Macbeth, *Fishdrum*
Soldier's Birthday, *The Literary Review*
Abortion, *New York Quarterly*
Suicide Note, *The Literary Review*
Sanctuary, in the book *Sacred Places* (Tokyo FM Japan)
Pay the Piper, *The Nassau Lit*
Heritage, *The Literary Review*
Dead Sea Trip, *The Notice*
Conceptions, *The Literary Review*
Bottle Caps, *The Literary Review*
No Fool Like a Young Fool, *The Nassau Lit*
Butterfly Lady, *The Literary Review*

About the Author

M. Z. Ribalow is a poet, playwright and author. His novel *Peanuts and Crackerjacks* and his new play *Masterpiece* are 2011 publications, and his short fiction appeared in an anthology on *Luck* in 2010. His two dozen plays have received some 180 productions in a dozen countries; four have been published. His work has been anthologized and has won prizes in London, New York, and regionally. He is series editor of the *Plays from New River* volumes (McFarland Publications) and has also co-written ten children's books and non-fiction books on sports, baseball and chess. He writes frequently on film, theatre, literature, music, and has appeared as a film historian on The Discovery Channel and on special feature documentaries of several DVD releases of classic films. He is Artistic Director and co-founder of New River Dramatists, which has for the last decade successfully developed hundreds of new plays and screenplays while discovering and nurturing gifted writers, and which also presents poetry, fiction and drama on the New River Radio Show on Art International Radio online. He lives in New York City, where he is currently full-time artist-in-residence at Fordham University.

NeoPoiesis: *a new way of making*

1) in ancient Greece, poiesis referred to the process of making: creation - production - organization - formation - causation

2) a process that can be physical and spiritual, biological and intellectual, artistic and technological, material and teleological, efficient and formal

3) a means of modifying the environment and a method of organizing the self, the making of art and music and poetry, the fashioning of memory and history and philosophy, the construction of perception and expression and reality

4) an independent publisher with a steadfast goal to print and promote outstanding poets, writers and artists that reflect the creative drive and spirit of the new electronic landscape

NeoPoiesisPress.com

www.ingramcontent.com/pod-product-compliance
Lightning Source LLC
LaVergne TN
LVHW091207080426
835509LV00006B/881